The Complete Network Marketing Boxset

How To Get Customers In Your Network Marketing Company

Network Marketing Selling Secrets

Internet Marketing For Network Marketers

Network Marketing Mindset

www.networkmarketingkingdom.com

Network Marketing Books

How To Get Customers In Your Network Marketing Company

Network Marketing Mindset

Network Marketing Selling Secrets

Internet Marketign For Network Marketers

How To Get Customers In Your Network Marketing Company

The Complete Guide To Converting Leads To Loyal Customers

By: Argena Olivis

www.networkmarketingkingdom.com

Bonus Video: How To Get Leads and Customers Online

Subscribe To Get Free Tips On How To Generate Leads and Get Customers

When you subscribe to get network marketing tips via email, you will get free access to exclusive subscriber-only resources. All you have to do is enter your email address to the right to get instant access.

These resources will help you get more out of your business – to be able to reach your goals, have more motivation, be at your best, and live the life you've always dreamed of. I'm always adding new resources, which you will be notified of as a subscriber. These will help you get an endless amount of leads and customers.

**Visit
www.networkmarketingkingdom.com/video
to Access The Bonus Video**

Table Of Contents

Introduction

I want to thank and congratulate you for reading the book, *"How To Get Customers In Your Network Marketing Company: The Complete Guide To Turning Leads Into Loyal Customers"* .

This book contains proven steps and strategies on how to generate leads and turn them into loyal customers.

Finding customers in your network marketing business is crucial for your success.

This is because it provides you with the comfort that you can actually sell the product and make a profit.

Once you know how to sell the product, it will be easier for you to train your team.

As network marketers, we need to see a profit right away in order to truly believe in the industry and stay involved in it.

Sales of your product give you that "right now" money. We need that "right now" money to invest in our marketing efforts and promote our opportunity.

In this book, you will learn the following:

- How to generate leads

- Having the right mindset

- How to turn leads into customers

- How to make your customers loyal to you

- How to increase your sales

- More lead generation strategies for both online and offline

As a business owner, you know that it's necessary to invest in yourself and in your business.

By purchasing this book, you are increasing your value. The more you study and take action, the more results you will see.

So learn how to generate leads and get more customers with these proven marketing strategies.

Thanks again for downloading this book, I hope you enjoy it!

Chapter 1: How To Generate Leads

Get Your Mindset Straight

Before we begin generating leads we need to make sure that you have the right mindset.

Network marketing is not an easy industry. But if you have a product you believe in, you should know in your heart and in your mind that you can be successful.

You have to be able to take rejection as a learning experience. If any of the strategies you take action on don't work for you, tweak them to make them work for you.

Your mindset has to be right. And you have to stay motivated and consistent to win.

Here are some tips on staying motivated daily:

- read for an hour a day (business or personal development books)

- watch YouTube videos on network marketing and motivation

- listen to business and network marketing podcasts

- work out and eat healthily

- have a daily routine and schedule and stay consistent

- set goals and do the work

- make a to-do list every night before bed

- read positive affirmations in the mirror

- create a vision board

- put a note or picture of the lifestyle you want to live on your laptop

Those are just examples of how to stay motivated. Do all that are suggested to you, or just one. But make sure you're not wasting your precious time.

Once your mindset is right, you can start generating leads.

So, have you done some of the suggested motivators above? I hope so. Now you're ready to move on and start generating leads.

How To Generate Leads

The number one thing you have to remember is that you ALWAYS want to get contact information.

If you don't get a person's contact information, you just lost a lead and a customer.

There are many ways to get a lead's contact information both online and offline without being invasive.

How To Get Leads Offline

To be honest, it's easier to build your customer base offline than online. This is because you're actually meeting people and talking to people.

People like seeing you to get a sense of trust for you.

Without trust, you cannot create a loyal customer base.

There are many strategies you can use to get leads offline:

- Vendor Shows
- Passive Advertising
- Job Fairs
- Flea Markets
- Tailgating
- Partnering With Stores
- Canvassing
- Parties

Vendor Shows

Vendor shows are shows that are created by organizations or individuals. They find vendors in the area and advertise the show to the public.

The vendors are usually private business owners or representatives from direct sales companies.

This is where vendors can set up a table and sell their products.

You can find vendor shows by Googling vendor shows in your area. Type in your city name, vendor shows, the month and the year you're looking to register for.

Make sure you look for shows in advance. Many of these shows get filled very quickly.

Once you get to the vendor show, it's time to collect leads.

You will be collecting leads by doing a giveaway. Giveaways are perfect for getting leads. It also gives you a reason to talk to people walking by your table.

Ask them if they'd like to enter to win.

Make your giveaways very appealing and put a time limit on it. By doing this it makes it seem more real.

For example: Tell them you're auctioning your giveaway off at 2pm when the vendor show is over.

Ask everyone if they want to enter to win your prize. If it's slow at the show, go around to each vendor and ask him or her if they'd like to enter.

It's great to make friends with other vendors so they can keep you updated with other shows they are doing.

So if you get a vendors contact info, add them on Facebook immediately so you can keep in touch.

Create a survey to collect contact information. The survey should be small enough that you can fold the piece of paper and put it in a basket for the raffle.

Below is an example of a survey that you can copy and paste in a word document and print out. It should print about two per page.

Replace the information in parenthesis so it is relevant to your company.

Are you currently being serviced by a (Your Company) Representative? YES _____ NO_____
I would like information about (check all that applies to you):
_____(Your Company) Partner/Helper (collect orders from friends, family, and co-workers,etc.)
_____Purchasing (Your Company) products
_____Receive future (Your Company) brochures
_____(Your Company) Fundraising (school, church, family reunion, other charity)
_____(Your Company) Earning Opportunity (starting my own (Your Company) business)

_____Hosting an Avon Party

THANK YOU for stopping by today

PLEASE PRINT ALL INFORMATION CLEARLY

NAME
_____

___

ADDRESS_____

_____

CITY/STATE/ZIP
_____

PHONE _____
EMAIL_____

As leads fill this out, fold up the paper and put it in the basket/jar.

If you're just getting to the show, put about three blank

ones in there so people will think that a lot of other people find your gift valuable.

People don't like to be the first ones; they like to follow the crowd. It's called "social proof".

Okay, so now you've collected a lot of contact info and you have some idea of what the person is interested in. So when you follow up with them you'll know what to talk to them about.

After the show is over, do your raffle. Most of the leads will have left by now. So just call the winner of your prize on the phone and let them know they won.

Passive Advertising

Passive advertising is another way to get leads, but these are not guaranteed. It's also not as effective as the other strategies. But, it's still worth your time.

Focus your time more on the other strategies, because those are the ones that will get you the most results.

The reason this method doesn't yield many results is because you're not collecting any contact information.

Here are some passive income strategies:

- tear-off fliers

- hanging information on door knobs

- leaving your business cards at the ATM, in library books, and in magazines

- Dropping your books/brochures places

Tear off flyers

Create tear-off flyers with your company's information and your contact information.

If interested, leads will be able to tear off one of the tabs on the flyer in order to take the contact information with them and call you later.

If you want to make the offer more appealing, tear off two of the tabs yourself, this will make people think it's a better offer.

Hanging information on doorknobs

In order to do this, you will need to have some of your company's promotional information such as books or flyers.

Put them in clear promotional bags that you're able to hang on doorknobs.

Go around your neighborhood and hang these on door knobs.

You can also use this method to hang your information other places like bathroom stalls, billboards, and more.

Get creative, the more information you get out there the more leads you'll generate.

Leaving Your Business Cards

Leave your business cards everywhere you go. You never know who's looking for what you have to offer.

Some great places to leave them consistently are: the ATM, in relevant library books, and in relevant magazines.

TIP Staple a sample of your product to your business card and hand it out to everyone. If you have a sample of your product attached you're more likely to get a call if they try the product.

Consistently do this and you will get a few calls. Every call counts. Just think, once you turn that lead into a customer, that can be worth hundreds of dollars in the future.

Dropping

The term "dropping" means you just leave your sales material somewhere for others to find.

This is another passive strategy, but it can still bring you in some leads.

You can drop sales materials in relevant local businesses, on the bus, doctor's offices, office buildings, and other places.

Job Fairs

Job fairs are not just for recruiting, you can also get some sales too. Most people won't want to join your company.

Many people at job fairs are looking for jobs, not to start a business.

But you don't have to lose out.

Collect their contact information by using the survey method outlined in the vendor show section.

Flea Markets

Flea markets are perfect because they are cheap, and the people there love to win free things.

You'll get a lot of leads by using the survey/raffle method outlined in the vendor show section.

Find local flea markets in your area by Googling.

Tailgating

This is a "best kept secret" method that many companies haven't gotten into.

Tailgating is great because you can collect leads right on the spot.

Tailgating is when you open your trunk and set up a "mini vendor show or job fair", and leads will stop by and see what you're giving away.

Create a sign that says "Free (your company's name)". Give out samples to anyone who stops by and asks what's free.

Make sure you're tailgating in an abandoned parking lot

or a shopping plaza that you have gotten permission from to do so.

Wherever you decide to tailgate, make sure it's in a busy place with a lot of traffic.

Use the survey/raffle method from the vendor shows section to collect leads.

Partnering with stores

Ask local businesses that are not in competition with your product if you can set up outside their store.

You're most likely to get a yes if you have something of value to offer them. The business is going to want to know what's in it for them.

Here are some ideas you can use to add value to a store when asking if you can set up outside:

- I will recommend your store to my customers

- I will do an employee appreciation for your workers

- I will do a customer appreciation and give out free samples to all the people that spend a certain amount in your store

- I will put your flyer in all of the promotional material I pass out

- I will not sell anything, I'll just talk about my business opportunity

- I can give you the names and emails of my customers

Once you get the okay to set up a table outside the business use the survey/raffle method outlined in the vendor show section.

Canvassing

Don't forget about old-fashioned canvassing. Go do-to-door and collect contact information.

You can do this by using the survey/raffle method, or just by simply asking for it and putting it in your phone.

This is the most up close and personal that way that you can get out of all of these results.

It's definitely worth a try. It depends on how bad you want it. Network marketing loves speed, and by canvassing, you will definitely be on the ball with leads.

Tell the lead about your product and how it can benefit them. How can you add value to them?

Make sure to leave them samples and promotional materials.

Let them know you're from their neighborhood and you're only a call away. This will build tons of trust.

Parties

Parties are another way to get leads. Pick a date to have a party, but make sure it's at least two weeks in advance.

Send out physical invitations to the people you want to invite. These can be current customers or people you want to become customers.

Next, create a Facebook event. If you know someone is active on social media and they have accepted your invite for your Facebook event, there is no need to send them a physical invitation too unless you want to.

Your invitations and Facebook event should have a number that guests can call to RSVP.

***Tip: Put a coupon in the invitation and on the Facebook event. Say if they bring a friend they get a free gift.

Follow up with the guests two days before the event and the day before the event to see if they still plan to attend.

Once you know how many people plan to attend make sure you have everything set for the party.

Create an agenda of what you want to go over, products you want to introduce, and games you want to play.

Remember to block out sometime in the middle of the party for people to place their orders. This ensures that if someone has to leave early you can still get his or her order.

A typical list of things you'll need for a party:

- order forms

- products to show

- samples

- gifts to give for prizes

- light refreshments

- pens/pencils and paper

- party games

- your agenda

Once you get some confirmed guests set up for your party. Make sure to have a sign-in sheet to collect leads. The sign in sheet should collect information similar to the vendor/raffle survey.

The Takeaway

Generating leads offline is pretty easy, but it's a time commitment. When going out advertising your business work it around your schedule.

Keep in mind that most people are out and about in the early mornings. So plan accordingly.

If you work a regular job, make the best out of your weekends.

Collect contact information whenever you can. Be creative, and invest in your business.

How To Get Leads Online

Getting leads online is a little harder if you don't have any internet marketing experience. But with these basic tips, you can successfully create leads online if you're consistent.

Take some of these tips and create a daily routine that

you can use to constantly generate leads.

Blog

Setting up a blog is fairly easy. But marketing it is a little more difficult due to the increasing number of blogs being made every single day.

First, you need to decide what you're going to blog about. Your blog should be marketed around the products your company promotes.

For example, if you're in a weight loss company your blog should be centered on something that will provide value such as healthy eating or weight loss.

Your goal is to provide value to your target lead so they will want to buy from you. But first you have to create trust, and that can take a while.

So find out what you're going to talk about. Make sure the subject of your blog helps people in some way. The best types of blogs are the kinds that teach people how to do something.

Once you've found how you're going to create value and market your product, register for a domain name.

After you buy your domain name, buy hosting. I recommend a service like Bluehost.

Once you have hosting, install WordPress. After that process, you're good to go.

If creating a blog is foreign to you I suggest searching for tutorials and YouTube videos that will walk you through the process step-by-step.

After you have your blog set up, this is when you should start creating valuable content.

There is a big learning curve to create a lead-generating website, but for now, just do what you know.

Set up a schedule for how often you will blog. Leads will want to hear from you often to create that bond.

Unfortunately, you cannot just put up a blog post and leads start pouring in. You have to market the blog.

This means you need to drive traffic to it from others sources such as social media, guest posting, writing books, building back-links, email marketing, and other methods.

Search Engine Optimization (SEO) is when you use keywords, which is where leads will be able to use these words and find your content through search engines.

Once you have some traffic it's time to put an email opt-in form on your blog so you can collect leads.

In order to do this, you'll need an email autoresponder like Aweber.

Once you have everything set up and you're creating content that is relevant to the products you sell, you should start getting leads.

Here are the types of posts you should create to get leads to your blog and onto your email list:

- how to posts (teaching leads how to do something relevant to your target market)

- tutorials (how to use the product you're selling)

- new updates regarding your product

- sales and promotions

After reading this section, if you truly want to learn how to generate leads through your blog make sure you study and learn how to get traffic and market your blog properly.

Instagram

Instagram is the newest social media platform that's owned by Facebook. But it's a great place to collect leads.

There are a lot of people from the younger generation using it, and it's growing every day.

In order to post on Instagram, you're going to need a smartphone to download the app. Or you can use a tablet.

You can view your profile through your desktop, but you cannot post that way.

To get leads on Instagram post the following:

- lifestyle pictures

- pictures of new products

- quote pictures

- funny pictures

- notes

- testimonials (before & after)

Post anything that will provide your viewers with entertainment and value. Start by following some people who promote products similar to what you have to offer.

Then follow the people that are following them. If people are following them this means they're interested in your product.

To get more followers and leads make sure to use hashtags. Hashtags are when you use the "#" sign in front of a word.

You want to use these so more people can find your posts.

Use hashtags relevant to the product you're promoting.

Twitter

To get leads on twitter make sure you're posting regularly and providing value in every post.

Post things like:

- tips

- tutorials

- quotes

- pictures

When following people, use the same techniques as Instagram, such as hashtags to promote your product.

Pinterest

Pinterest is another new social media site but it can still bring in plenty of leads. Pinterest is more of a visual site. So all you'll be posting is pictures.

Create boards that are eye-catching and relevant to your product. Pin all the pictures from both your blog and company website.

You can also use hashtags on Pinterest.

YouTube

YouTube is one of the best ways to get leads online fast. This is because video outdoes all other forms of lead generation.

Creating a valuable video that will help your target market is a great strategy.

Here are some types of YouTube videos you can create:

- tutorials

- product reviews

- giveaways

Optimize your YouTube videos so you'll get maximum exposure.

To increase your conversions, make sure to use the proper keywords in the title, description, and tags so you'll rank in Google and in the search engines.

Have fun on your channel and use YouTube to bring traffic to your products.

Promote Your Company Website

We had a lot of talk about creating your own blog but don't forget about the one that your network marketing company provides for you.

There should be a lot of links going out from your blog to your company website. Use website links to promote specific products so they can buy right from your site.

Always link to your site and promote your site on your business card, social media, and anywhere else you see fit.

eBooks

Create eBooks relevant to your product and target market. In the eBook put an opt-in offer to collect leads.

eBooks are also a great way to promote your blog or company website.

The content in your eBook should teach your leads how to do something. Once they find value in what you have taught them they will want to become your customers.

Take Away

Use one or more of these strategies when creating leads online. As I've mentioned, generating leads online is harder than offline.

It will take time and patience, but it will work if you stick to it.

To save yourself time from being in front of the computer all of the time use systems to automate your online efforts.

For social media, use systems like Hootsuite.

You're able to schedule blog posts and YouTube videos to go out in the future.

Use batching to automate this process. Create a lot of content and schedule it for the week.

You can also have emails going out to your leads automatically with your email software.

Remember to focus on your target market. Your target market is whom you will be focusing on selling to.

Set updates in your planner for when you will be writing posts and posting on social media.

Make a daily routine to promote your company's website on different sites. Post in relevant forums to create leads.

In Conclusion

You now have learned how to generate leads online and offline. Put these strategies into action and start getting some results.

In the next chapter, we will discuss how to turn those leads into customers.

Chapter 2: How To Turn Leads Into Customers

Generating leads is great, but that's not where the money is. You get money when you turn your leads into customers.

This is a simple process that will increase your sales and conversions if you take action.

Following Up

You can generate leads all day, but if you don't follow up all your effort was for nothing.

You have to follow up to make the money. That's just the way it works.

Following up with leads offline

When you've done passive prospecting and you've gotten results, you will start getting calls from leads without having to follow up with them.

These leads are automatically customers because if they're calling you, it's so they can place an order.

As far as the raffle/survey from leads that you've gotten from job fairs, vendor shows, etc., you will have to call them and follow up with them.

Call them the next day, tell them how nice it was to meet them and ask them if they'd like a sample.

Don't call and ask for the order right off the bat. You first want to build a rapport.

If your company has an email database where it sends its own emails or has an address book, upload these contacts into that database the same day you get the info or as soon as possible.

Following up with leads online

This won't take a lot of your effort. Use autoresponders to send out promotional and helpful emails.

The system itself will do the conversion. If you're providing enough value, the leads on your email list will become your customers.

Consistency

This is where you start using your planner. Have a follow-up day where you call customers and see if they'd like to order anything. This can be when a new product has launched or when you think they will have run out of the product.

Constantly follow up with leads. Call them as soon as possible. Be polite and professional when making calls.

If you do this over and over again you're bound to convert many of your leads into customers.

Planning

Plan how many leads you will call and when you will call them.

Set goals for how many customers you will get a week. Make the process fun and simple.

Take away

The key to turning leads into customers is following up.

Follow up with all the leads you collect as soon as possible.

Chapter 3: How To Make Customers Loyal

Getting a customer is not easy and neither is creating a loyal one. But creating loyal customers is what will truly make you rich.

A customer is great, but a customer that orders from you, and only you all the time is priceless.

Customer List

A customer list is a list of people that has purchased something from you that you are going to want to follow up with.

Use this list to keep track of who got your latest brochures/sales material.

Also use this list to keep track of who ordered when and when you think they'll need a refill/new product.

You'll have access to a printable customer list to keep you organized later.

The point of this list is to keep track and check off names once you've given them your updated sales material.

Also, check off names when you have followed up with a customer about ordering a product.

Customers will be impressed about how you remembered them, and they won't mind your follow up call.

Thank you cards

Send and/or put thank you cards in customer orders.

If a customer orders from you make sure to thank them every single time.

You can send an email, mail a thank you card, or put it in their order.

This simple gesture will win over customers and make them loyal to you. Most network marketers don't think to do this.

**TIP: Thank you cards are even more special when they're handwritten.

Samples

Your customers absolutely love samples. This is also a great way to introduce a new product to your customers to raise your sales.

You shouldn't mind investing in samples for customers that have already spent money with you. This means that you'll be getting your sample investment back time and time again.

Contests

Stir up some fun with your customer base by doing a contest. You can raffle off a product if they spend a certain amount in your store or you could have a customer of the month contest.

It doesn't matter the contest just make it fun and get all your customers involved.

***TIP: A good contest to have is to see what customers can get you the most referrals

Following Up

Make the follow up a pleasant experience for your customers. Mention how you're thankful that they've purchased from you.

Mention what products they've purchased previously, and if you can get them a better deal, then do it.

Know What Your Customer Likes

Be mindful of what your customers like so if the item goes on sale you can let them know.

They will truly appreciate the effort in trying to save them money on their favorite items.

Also, if a product similar to what they like comes out you'll be able to recommend the product to them.

Monthly Newsletter

Send your entire customer base monthly newsletters. Don't just send one when there's a sale or promotion.

When sending out your monthly newsletters make sure to have a theme around it. You can choose a holiday for that month or just something fun.

Your customer list can be mailed out physically or sent in an email.

What to include in the monthly newsletter:

- customer of the month

- sales and deals

- coupons

- new products that will be launching

- links back to your social media and blog

- product recommendations

- tutorials on how to use products

- new ideas

- etc.

Add things to your newsletter that will make your customer excited to receive it.

Gifts

Everyone loves gifts. Send your customers gifts. These gifts can be digital or physical.

Make the gift presentable and fun. Also, make sure you add a note for why they are receiving the gift.

Appropriate times to send customers gifts:

- samples of new products

- incentive for ordering online

- birthdays and anniversaries

- holidays

- just because (have a random customer receive a gift every month)

Because of your kindness customers will be loyal to you and excited to shop with you again.

Over deliver

No matter what you do, always over deliver. Go way beyond your customer's expectations and they will never buy from anyone else.

Over deliver on everything: your newsletters, your customer service, the content on your blog and social media, absolutely everything!

When a customer is used to your high-quality customer service, they will stick with you, recommend you, and love you.

Chapter 4: Increase Your Sales

Increasing your sales will be super easy once you know how to generate leads and turn those leads into loyal customers.

But here are some ideas that will maximize your results.

Goal Setting

Set sales goals for yourself. Whether you want to make extra income, supplement your income, or fully replace your income, you're going to need goals.

Weekly goals are perfect when it comes to sales. Have weekly goals of how many leads you want, customers you want, and sales you want.

Every commission scale for network marketing companies is different.

Say you get 40% profit on each sale you make and your best selling product is $20. How many $20 products would you have to sell to make the income you want?

Do the math! This is crucial. You have to do the math so you know exactly how much you need to make to reach your goals.

After you do the math for how much you need to sell, you need to subtract any business related expenses.

Your business expenses may be:

- promotional materials (books/brochures/pamphlets)

- samples

- gifts

- vendor shows

- flea markets

- paper for fliers and ink

- business cards

- stamps and stickers

- crafts

- etc.

Whatever you purchased that week that was business related subtract it from the total you earned.

Keeping track of this on a weekly basis will help you to form a habit of recording and tracking.

It's best to do this in an excel document or an app of some sort.

Once you know how much the average expenses are for each week you can subtract it from your total automatically so you'll know exactly how much you plan to make.

If you really want to get on track, budget your samples and sales materials.

For example: Have a $20/month budget for samples ($5/wk).

TIPSet a goal for how much you plan to make weekly.

Work Hard

Have you ever heard the saying it's called net "work" marketing not net "lazy" marketing?

Well, the saying is true.

Get out there: invest in yourself and your business. Network marketing not only increases your money but it also increases your confidence.

You will find it easier to talk to others, and you will truly grow as a person.

Set up your daily routine for success, and get out there and work your plan.

Get Your Name Out There

You truly have to market your business daily to see success.

Get out there and create partnerships with other entrepreneurs.

You can truly scale up your business by knowing the right people in the right places.

Someone with more influence can take you to the next level. So always be getting your name out there.

Maximize Finding Leads

Finding leads is an income producing activity.

You should be spending most of your time following up with leads because they can potentially become your customers.

The more leads the better. If you see a shortage of customers, go out a and generate more leads and convert them.

Be The "Go To" Person For Your Product

If someone asks about a specific product, and you're selling it, your name should come to their mind.

The company you are in is already branded, that's what corporate does.

But you have to brand yourself to be the go-to person for your product. When they think of "(insert your product name here)" they should think of you.

Find every single thing you can do to dominate the niche for the product you sell.

You have to get yourself out there. Do video tutorials, product demonstrations, product reviews, and the whole nine.

You have to know your products, and how to use them.

Invest Back Into Your Business

Once you start making more money because of your increased sales, it's time to scale up your business.

Invest back into your business and into yourself.

The more your increase your skills, the more you will increase your sales.

Invest in more training and materials for your business. You will get your investment back ten times over if you continue to work hard and take action on what you learn.

Chapter 5: More Lead Generation Strategies

Lead generation is going to be what keeps your business going. If you run out of people to talk to, you will get frustrated and quit.

This is why I added more strategies on how to generate leads both online and offline.

Lead Generation Offline

Your offline efforts are just as important as your online efforts. In the beginning, you should be building your customer base both on and offline for maximum results.

Then once you generate enough customers online and you want to continue to work from home you can convert your offline customers to online customers.

Warm Market

Your warm market is the people you know. Make sure to tap into this market for sales; they will be your main customers.

Call every person in your phone and ask if it'd be okay if you send him or her a sample or book/brochure/pamphlet. Then follow up with them.

Your warm marketing is where you'll get most of your sales from at first. It's a great place to start but if you want to make money always expand.

Cold Market

Your cold market is going to be a little harder to convince. This is why you need to make sure they're also your target market.

Your target market is the people who are actively searching for your products, solutions to your products, or have a need for your product.

Once you meet these people and get their contact information at vendor shows, flea markets, and job fairs make sure to follow up with them.

Local Chamber of Commerce

Make sure to register at your local chamber of commerce. This is not free but it will get you updates on the local events.

You'll also get to meet lots of other people who can become leads if you get their information.

Community

You should be the go-to person for your product in your community. If there are other people that sell in your community and are not on your team, you should be the one who your neighbors go to.

Totally dominate your community. Market you're business so everyone knows what you do and want to buy from you.

Lead Generation Online

Online is truly what you want to strive for. But in the beginning don't be too lazy to go offline and do what you have to do.

Message Facebook Friends

Send a message to your Facebook friends who can use your product. Ask them "would it be okay if I give you a sample of "(your product)"?

They will say yes. Make sure you get them some samples A.S.A.P. and follow up with them within two days. Ask how they liked the sample and if you can get them a "book/brochure/pamphlet".

Pay Per Click Ads

Pay per click advertising is another way you can generate leads. This method is mainly used for those who have a bigger budget when starting out.

If your budget allows, look into advertising on Google or on Facebook.

Chapter 6: Get To Work

In this book you have learned how to:

- generate leads

- turn leads into customers

- make your customers loyal

- increase your sales

- generate leads online and offline

- stay motivated

Now all you have to do is put what you learn into action and you will have success if you do.

Reading is great, but it will get you nowhere if you don't apply what you read.

I truly want you to get out there and test these strategies because they do work if you do.

You deserve a business and the financial freedom that comes along with it. If you want it bad enough you will truly implement this information and go to the top!

Now go out there, generate some leads, and most importantly... follow up. Will you be the next network marketing success story?

Work on your mindset daily and create a daily routine for your business.

We are defined by our habits. Have habits of working smart and hard.

Conclusion

Thank you again for reading this book!

I hope this book was able to help you to get more customers in your network marketing company.

The next step is to go out and generate some leads.

Finally, if you enjoyed this book, then I'd like to ask you for a favor. Would you be kind enough to leave a review for this book on Amazon? It'd be greatly appreciated!

By leaving a review you help other marketers find the book and it also gives me feedback on the book; your review will let me know what I can improve on or what I've done well.

Thank you and good luck!

Network Marketing Selling Secrets

50 Ways To Get New Customers

www.networkmarketingkingdom.com

Bonus Video: How To Get Leads and Customers Online

Subscribe To Get Free Tips On How To Generate Leads and Get Customers

When you subscribe to get network marketing tips via email, you will get free access to exclusive subscriber-only resources. All you have to do is enter your email address to the right to get instant access.

These resources will help you get more out of your business – to be able to reach your goals, have more motivation, be at your best, and live the life you've always dreamed of. I'm always adding new resources, which you will be notified of as a subscriber. These will help you get an endless amount of leads and customers.

Visit
www.networkmarketingkingdom.com/video
to Access The Bonus Video

Introduction

I want to thank you and congratulate you for reading the book, *"Network Marketing Selling Secrets: 50 Ways To Get New Customers"*.

This book contains 50 proven ways to get customers in your network marketing company.

If you're looking for fresh ideas on how to increase your sales this week, look no further.

You will find some unique ways to increase your customer base; as well as some ways you may have heard of before but never took action on.

Discover how getting customers both online and offline will increase you and your team's chances for success.

Many networkers are using the same strategies. You want to plant seeds in many different ways so you'll always have a stream of new customers coming in.

Learn how to master one way of getting customers, and move on to master another. Once you find out what's working best, use and improve that strategy to make it even better.

If you take action on these selling secrets, you will already be ahead of most-- because most people don't take action.

Don't you think it's time you start putting in the work necessary to live the lifestyle you want?

We all want more time with the family, and the freedom to do what we want whenever we want without money being an object.

You cannot make money without others; so it's best to try to help as many people as you can, and always add value so people will be willing to pay you.

Your goal should be: to be the "go to" person for your product; to win customers over so they are loyal to you and recommend you to their friends and family.

If you're not making money or getting any customers, it may be because you're not adding enough value. But through these selling strategies; I'll show you how to do so.

I'm sure you got into network marketing because you wanted something better.

Well, in this book is an opportunity to create more freedom in your life by making more money in your business.

Thanks again for reading *Network Marketing Selling Secrets*, I hope you enjoy it!

guarantee assurance.

Table Of Contents

Chapter 1: Ways To Get Customers Offline

First, we are going to go into ways to get customers offline. Getting customers offline can be known as active marketing.

This means you are actively engaging with people and meeting people.

Active marketing is the fastest way to get new customers when trying to get customers online it takes time to build a trusting relationship.

A lot of people miss the one-to-one communication with those they are buying from.

Therefore, your chances of getting customers offline are very high.

This book is intended to help you find new customers. But remember that it's harder to find new customers than to get returning customers.

So after you've found some new customers make sure to have outstanding customer service so they'll always return back to you, and only you.

Way #1: Vendor Shows

Vendor shows are events put on by organizations or other small business owners like yourself.

I'm big on vendor shows because I got a lot of leads this way.

To get customers at vendor shows, you don't necessarily need to have product on hand-- but that is ideal.

When a potential customer approaches your table, make sure to be very welcoming.

Have a form there for them to fill out where they can be entered into a giveaway. You always want to collect contact information, no matter what.

Offer them something. Give them a sample.

If you have products on hand to sell, be knowledgeable about them and answer all their questions.

If they end up buying something from you, make sure to put your sales material or business card in their shopping bag.

Also, make sure to collect their contact information by having them fill out a raffle ticket or document.

Keep notes about new customer names, and what they purchased from you. Then follow up with them in a few days and ask how they're enjoying whatever they purchased.

If they don't purchase anything, still make it your business to meet them and get to know them a little better.

So if they take a sample, you can follow up with them later to ask they enjoyed the sample.

Way #2: Flea Markets

Flea markets are similar to vendor shows. Find flea

markets in your area by searching in Google.

If you're constantly at a particular flea market, customers may get used to seeing you there and recommend you to their friends.

The best way to win at a flea market is to be consistent in showing up there.

Also, keep in mind that many people go to flea markets to get discounted items.

You may want to entice a lead by offering them lower priced items, items that others have returned, or a discount you've made up yourself.

Way #3: Sales Material Drop

This is when you leave your sales material or promotional material for your company in high traffic areas or places you know people are waiting to get service.

Many companies have some type of books or pamphlets that they give out, or that the consultants have to buy, that lets customers know more about the product or to showcase the products they offer.

If your company doesn't offer this, create your own documents.

When I say drop, that basically means "leave". So leave your sales material in places such as doctors' offices, local businesses, and any other places that people are waiting to get serviced.

Way #4: Hanging Sales Materials On Doorknobs

Hanging your promotional materials on doorknobs is a great way to increase your customer base.

Simply put your sales material in clear bags that will fit nicely and look professional on a door knob and leave them at houses in your neighborhood.

Do this a few times around your neighborhood until you start getting results. Then move on and expand your reach into different areas.

Way #5: Business Appreciation

Call businesses that have employees that may be interested in what product you sell.

Tell them that they were nominated your business of the week. Ask if you can stop by and give everyone in the office free samples.

When you go to drop off the samples make sure to have your sales material with you. This will also be a good time to do a raffle.

Have the people in the office fill out the raffle forms, you come back for the forms at a later date. Now you have successfully collected names, emails, and possibly phone numbers.

Make sure to follow up with all the people who have entered into your raffle to see if they liked the samples.

Way #6: Meet Ups

Find groups in your city that you are interested in. It doesn't matter what type of group it is. Make some friends and simply tell them what you do.

They may be interested or know someone who is interested in your products.

You can go to www.meetup.com to find these groups.

Way #7: Garage sales

Host a garage sale, or find out if someone in your family or your friends will be having one anytime soon.

Make sure to put out your sales materials, samples, and products you have on hand.

Many people love garage sales, and it'll be another way to get your name out there.

Way #8: Local Chamber of Commerce

Sign up for your local chamber of commerce.

They will let you know when there's meetings in your area, and you'll get the heads up on events that are happening in your neighborhood.

Way #9: Parties

Host a party. Or have someone else host a party.

You can have it at your place or rent out an area. Either way, make it happen.

If you see that you're getting customers this way, start hosting more parties.

Way #10: Employee Appreciation

Contact businesses and ask them if you can set up an employee appreciation for them.

Do something nice for the employees that work for their company. For example: If you sell weight loss products then give each employee a free consultation.

Way #11: Set Up Outside or Inside of Businesses

Ask local businesses if you can do a customer appreciation for them. When you set up your table give out something to the people approaching the store or leaving the store.

When contacting businesses owners, let them know what's in it for them. Tell them you'll be giving out free items to customers, or that you'll give discounts to the customers who buy something from their business.

Also, tell them to keep in mind that you'll be trying to get customers in the door.

Way #12: Advertising

Depending on your budget you can start advertising. Consider doing a billboard or putting up a yard sign in your yard.

Any exposure is great, make sure to always leave a business card or fliers in local businesses that allow it.

Way #13: Sample Packs

Sample packs are packs that you create using samples and other goodies. Buy professional looking plastic bags from the dollar store and put samples, a business card, a fund-raising flier, and candy in them.

Hand them out the people while doing errands or when you're just out and about.

Way #14: Business Cards In Books

Go to the library and look for the book section that is relevant to the product you're trying to sell. Put your business cards in all the books.

You can also do the same thing in bookstores.

If you do this method, make sure to have your company

website on your cards.

I remember someone actually contacted me after finding my businesses card in a book. It was like 6 months after the fact.

Way #15: Business Cards at ATM

Leave your business cards at the ATM. Also, leave it at gas stations.

Way #16: Consultations

Offer free consultations to people that may be able to benefit from your product.

Way #17: Post Cards

Send out postcards to people in your area letting them know that you are the one representing your company in that area.

There are services that tell you all the addresses in the neighborhood and will also send out the card for you.

Way #18: Canvassing

Go door to do and let people know what you do and what you have to offer.

Be careful, make sure not to do this alone.

Way #19: Fundraising

Set up fundraisers with customers.

Seek out groups that can benefit from doing fundraisers such as school groups and clubs in your area.

Way #20: Raffles

Sell raffle tickets and auction off your products at different events.

Or do raffles with existing customers, tell your customers that for every customer they refer to you, they'll get another raffle ticket for free to put in the pot.

Way #21: Coupons

Create coupons and give them out to potential customers.

Also, offer your own sales on your products.

Offer a discount to first-time customers.

Way #22: Open House

Host an open house. An open house will require you to have products on hand.

Allow people to come in and view what products you have to offer, and buy them.

Also, let them know of upcoming products so they can pre-order.

You can do this at your place with your warm market. Or you can do it at a local place in the community and allow the general public to attend.

Make sure to advertise this well, it's more likely for people to show up for a party than an open house.

Be sure to give out samples and sample packs.

Way #23: Phone Calls To Warm Market

Make phone calls to your warm market. Your warm market is your family, friends, and associates.

Let them know you're in business. Chances are they'll buy from you, or help you to get customers.

Way #24: Referrals

The best way to get referrals is to have outstanding customer service. Make your customer service so outstanding that people can't wait to share the experience with others.

As I've mentioned before, it's easier to get an existing customer to order from you again than to get a new one.

Create a loyal customer base by: returning calls and emails in a timely manner, saying thank you every time, following up with them, knowing what they like, etc.

Way #25: Advertising

Advertise your company. Always wear your company logo, use car signs, name tags, bags/purses, etc.

Chapter 2: Ways To Get Customers Online

In order to get customers online, you may have to learn some internet marketing. If you master a few of these ways, it's possible that you can go online completely and make money from home.

To get customers online you have to be super disciplined and consistent. You can do it, but it will take time.

If you don't have a lot of time, you can outsource a lot of these tasks. Consider hiring a virtual assistant to do your social media management.

Way #26: Facebook

This is most likely where most of your potential customers are hanging out. It's the biggest social media platform-- almost everyone has a Facebook.

Create a Facebook Business Page/Fan Page. And create a Facebook Group.

Share valuable and relevant content on your page. Keep in mind social media is used for building relationships-- it's not a place to spam your website link everywhere.

Be very strategic about how you will provide value to your fans.

Share things such as:

- images

- quotes

- videos

- blog posts

- events

- lifestyle

- tips

If you offer valuable and likable content on your page--people will buy from you, or buy from you again.

You can create images using different apps on your phone or using services such as www.picmonkey.com or www.canva.com. The app I use to create quote images on my phone is called Word Swag.

Update your page regularly and be yourself.

Way #27: YouTube

I'm willing to bet most of the people in your company are not doing videos on YouTube.

Some may be, most are not.

This is a great way to stand out to your customers.

Create videos that will help them such as tutorials, demonstrations, or reviews.

Let them know when sales are going on.

Allow people to connect with you through your videos, create some videos about your lifestyle or day in the life.

Always remember to market your Facebook Fan Page in your YouTube description. Also, post your new videos to your Facebook pages.

Way #28: Google +

Google + is another way to get customers. Make sure to make use of hashtags.

Hashtags are when you put a "#" sign in front of a keyword that you want to be found for.

Post your YouTube Videos to Google +.

Way #29: Pinterest

Pinterest is a very visual social media platform. Many women use this site.

Pinterest is basically all images, but you can also add YouTube videos.

Get customers by marketing your products, sales, discounts, and promo codes.

Make use of hashtags too.

You can even take pictures of blog posts or other offers your running in order to entice customers to shop at your store.

Way #30: Website

Create a website to promote your business. Make sure you are following your company's terms and conditions.

Your best bet is to create a website around the product you sell.

Provide value by helping people solve problems.

You can use this website to drive traffic to your company site where they can purchase products.

You can also use your website to create another income stream through advertising, product creation, email marketing, and affiliate marketing.

For a step-by-step tutorial on how to create a website go to http://www.networkmarketingkingdom.com/website/

Way #31: Email Marketing

Use email marketing software like Aweber to collect names and emails online.

By building an email list you, can send your customers emails about offers and let them know why they should shop with you instead of the other distributors in your company.

Provide your subscribers with valuable content that is relevant.

In turn, your customers will grow to like and trust you.

Visit http://www.argenaolivis.com/email-marketing-101/ for step by step instructions on how to get started with email marketing.

Way #32: Yahoo Answers

Yahoo Answers is a hidden jewel, and many markers haven't tapped into this strategy yet.

Look for people asking questions related to the products you sell. Offer them help.

Leave thorough answers to questions. Personalize the answer by using the person's first name.

Stand out and really provide that person with value. Then leave a link back to your website or your online store.

Make your yahoo profile stands out by adding a picture of yourself and links to ways that people can get in touch with you.

There's also a section on your profile that allows you to fill out personal questions about yourself, answer these. If you decide to make this one of your strategies, answer questions daily. You can be ranked higher if people vote your question as the best answer.

You get points for just signing in to answer questions too.

Way #33: Instagram

Instagram is a social media platform that can bring you a lot of business if used in the right way.

To be successful on Instagram, make use of hashtags (like on Google Plus). Instagram requires the use of their app to post pictures. So make sure to download the app on your phone.

Facebook actually owns Instagram, and it's really becoming very popular for marketers, especially the younger generation.

Post pictures and very short videos on Instagram to engage your audience.

If you put hashtags under your images and videos you are more likely to be found. When people enjoy what you're posting they have the opportunity to follow you.

When posting hashtags, don't put them directly in the post; put them in a comment beneath your post. This allows you to delete and add tags at a later time without having to take down the entire post.

Another trick is to use your location settings as a call to action. For example, in the location settings you can put "click the link in bio".

The things that work best on Instagram are:

- inspirational quote images

- personal lifestyle images

- quick videos that give out tips

You can also use Instagram to market your blog and products.

You are only allowed one "clickable link", and that's in your author bio. My suggestion would be to put your store link up.

Way #34: Guest Posting

Guest post on blogs. Guest posting is when you write an article for a popular blog in your niche.

It will be on someone else's blog, but if that blogger is getting traffic, you may be able to grow your own audience and in turn get more customers.

After the blog or before the blog, the blogger allows you to add information about yourself and where people can find you at online. Sometimes they'll even allow you to put a link to your squeeze page or landing page so you can grow your email list.

This is a great opportunity to send more traffic to your website or store.

The first step is to find a popular blog that is related to the products you sell. Then email the blogger and ask if you can do a guest blog on their site.

Make sure your blog post is super high quality so people will want to connect with you.

Way #35: Squidoo

Squidoo.com is a place where you can post articles on a blogging platform that's already getting traffic.

Use the right keywords and make sure the article you write is relevant to the product you sell.

You are allowed to put links back to your website or store.

Just like guest posting, if the article is quality people will want to learn more about what you have to offer.

Way #36: SlideShare

SlideShare is a place that you can create a group of slides that inform people on a particular topic of your choosing.

Create a slide show presentation that tells someone how to do something. Then make sure to put a link back to your products or website.

Make sure to use relevant keywords in your title and throughout the presentation.

Way #37: Twitter

Twitter is one of the more popular social media platforms, you most likely already have an account.

The great thing about Twitter is that it's a live search engine. So whatever phrase you search for on Twitter, you can find people talking about that subject in real time.

This is great for getting customers. Do a search for some of the products you have and see if someone is talking about purchasing or looking for a "good one".

For example: If your company sells lipstick: Search for "lipstick" in the Twitter search bar and see if anyone is looking for a recommendation. If they are saying things like "need a new lipstick" then follow them and start a conversation with them. Do not try to sell to them, just try to help solve their problem. So in this situation, you may want to say something like "oh, what kind do you usually get."

Keep in mind that this is another great place to use hashtags. And to really get noticed, talk about what's trending.

Way #38: Advertise On Websites

This will take a money investment, but can be well worth it. Have the right mindset. Don't think about how much it's going to cost you, think about how much it's going to make you.

Look to advertise on sites that are talking about something relevant to the company you're in.

If the site is getting a lot of visitors, ask the owner how much it costs to advertise on their website.

Sometimes they will already have a page that discusses how much it costs to advertise.

It's just your job to test this strategy out and see how much return you get from it.

Way #39: Forums

Join and participate in forums that are similar to the type of company you are in.

Help people out in the forums, similar to the strategy with Yahoo Answers.

The more helpful you are to someone, the more likely they are to check out what you have to offer.

Just provide people with information and help people out as much as you can.

What goes around, comes around.

Way #40: Directories

Submit your business website to directories online.

People look at directories to find different websites they are looking for.

There are some free ones and some paid ones.

Way #41: Webinars

Host a webinar to get customers. Webinars are like seminars, but online.

Provide them with valuable information that is related to your product and put on a live show to help them with what they're struggling with.

Webinars can be live or recorded.

After you have provided the valuable information, sell your products at the end.

I'm sure there are not many people in your company using this strategy-- this is a great way to get ahead!

Way #42: E-Parties

Host a party online.

You can do this by creating a Facebook event or group.

You can set it up to where if people order from your website between a certain window of time, they get a discount.

There are many ways to do this. Create a video, do a live webinar, or just provide them with all the information on Facebook.

You can really host the party anywhere online. Just have a start time and end time and give people a reason to want to "come" to the party.

Way #43: Giveaways

Host a giveaway on your YouTube channel.

This is also a way to get more Facebook likes, get people on your email list, or get traffic to your store.

When you do a giveaway, offer a product or a product bundle people will really want.

Give the people directions on what they have to do to "enter to win".

The great thing about this is only one person wins, and you still have collected leads.

People may go back to your store and order the product even if they don't win.

Have a start date and end date. Tell viewers when you're going to be selecting the winner and do a follow-up video.

Way #44: Contests

Contests are another way to expand your customer base.

You can make the contest relevant to your product line.

For example: If you sell weight loss products then you can do a "lose 10 pounds in a month" contest. Whoever wins give them something cool.'

With this, you can either draw a name or give everyone who has won a prize. It doesn't have to be a physical prize. You can give out an eBook or something else digital.

But this is a great way to promote your products and build a community while having fun.

Way #45: Promo Codes/ Sales / Discounts

People love to save money. Always make it known when you offer free shipping or promo codes that can save your customers a few bucks.

These are great because they have an end date, which will inspire the customer to take action right away.

Way #46: eBook

Write an eBook relevant to what you sell.

You can charge for it or make it free for those who opt-in to your email list.

From there you can promote your products if it will help them to solve a particular problem they're struggling with.

Get my free course on how to create a kindle book by visiting: http://www.argenaolivis.com/freekindlecourse

Way #47: PPC

Use a pay per click campaign with an advertising company.

The advertising company will show your ads to prospects, and you can have a link straight to your store, to your website, or to your email list.

You can also do a Facebook Ads campaign.

Paid traffic is something to truly consider these days. Although, if you're consistent with getting free traffic, then that's great.

But paid traffic gives you more security. Once you know the numbers, how much it costs to acquire a customer, you're already winning the game.

There are many advertising companies, you don't have to go with any big ones like Google Adwords. But regardless of whatever company you choose, I highly recommend taking a course on it first so you don't waste a ton of money.

Way #48: Testimonials

Use testimonials from people that have used your product and tell people about it through your blog, eBooks, ads, or wherever you market online.

People are more likely to invest in things they see are getting results.

You can also use testimonials from your current customers about your outstanding customer service. This will set you apart from others.

Also, use things such as before and after photos on your social media.

Way #49: Product Demos

Product demonstrations are another way to get customers.

Walk customers through the entire process step-by-step on how to use your products.

You can do this through videos, blog posts, emails,

eBooks, etc.

Post product demos to your social media and promote them on your website.

This will show that you know what you're doing, and you will be seen as an expert on whatever you're selling.

Way #50: Referrals/Getting Content Shared

When you share amazing content online, people will begin to notice.

Post things that you yourself would share.

This could be things like inspiring pictures, uplifting messages, or just something funny.

Be shareable online and you begin to see profits come in.

Sometimes it's best to ask for the share. Tell your fans to share a piece of content and give them a reason to.

Chapter 3: Piecing It All Together

In order to get customers, you're going to have to pick only a few ways and see which ways are giving you the biggest return on your investment.

So right now, write down the two ways you will start to get customers.

Although we've gone over 50 ways to get customers, focus is still important so you can make sure you're being super productive and efficient every day.

It's called the 80/20 rule; 20% of what you do will result in 80% of your customers.

So remember to focus, focus on one company and about two strategies and see how they work for you.

Then set up a game plan. For example: How many vendor shows do you want to do next week, how often are you willing to post on Facebook, etc.

Create your game plan and set goals for what you plan on doing. Then, starting today-- take action on the strategies and see what results you get.

If you see a strategy not working after 3 weeks or so, drop it and move on to the next.

Online, some strategies may take longer-- but you are planting seeds and many of the things you post, such as videos, will always be up to collect leads for you no matter what you are doing and where you are, and for years to come.

You never know what a potential customer's situation is, they may come back next week after they get paid and give you a call or shop at your store online.

Give it time, it will require patience, but it also requires consistency.

Be consistent

If you find that a strategy works, do more of it and be consistent with it.

No matter the strategy, you should have a set schedule for when you are going to prospect for customers.

Stick to it, and you're bound to see results.

My recommendation is to focus on only two strategies in a given week. This will let you know how well it's working and if you should ramp it up, or slow it down.

Referrals

Referrals are the best customers because you get them without having to go out and search for them.

Have outstanding customer service, and your referral rate will sky rocket!

All in all, you do have what it takes to be successful. Consistent action will get you the results!

The Takeaway

Work on your mindset, because in this business, if you don't believe you can do it; unfortunately, you won't get far.

Invest in yourself. Educate yourself and focus on self-growth.

Never come from a selfish place, always be thinking how you can serve your customers and fans better.

Have an abundance mindset, there's plenty of customers to go around. Mastermind with like-minded people and find a mentor.

Manage your money well, and make sure you're turning a profit in your business. Take this seriously and you will succeed!

I'm happy that you got to the end of this book. I have given you 50 proven ways to get customers. What will you do with the information?

Success= Take action, get some results, share the results, repeat.

Conclusion

Thank you again for reading *Network Marketing Selling Secrets*!

I hope this book was able to help you to find strategies that will increase your customer base.

The next step is to use one of these strategies and take consistent action.

Finally, if you enjoyed this book, then I'd like to ask you for a favor, would you be kind enough to leave a review for this book on Amazon? It'd be greatly appreciated!

Thank you and good luck!

Internet Marketing For Network Marketers

How To Create Automated Systems To Get Recruits and Customers Online

www.networkmarketingkingdom.com

Bonus Video: How To Get Leads and Customers Online

Subscribe To Get Free Tips On How To Generate Leads and Get Customers

When you subscribe to get network marketing tips via email, you will get free access to exclusive subscriber-only resources. All you have to do is enter your email address to the right to get instant access.

These resources will help you get more out of your business – to be able to reach your goals, have more motivation, be at your best, and live the life you've always dreamed of. I'm always adding new resources, which you will be notified of as a subscriber. These will help you get an endless amount of leads and customers.

Visit
www.networkmarketingkingdom.com/video
to Access The Bonus Video

Table Of Contents

Introduction

I want to thank you and congratulate you for reading the book, *"Internet Marketing for Network Marketers: How To Create Automated Systems To Get Recruits And Customers Online"*.

This book contains proven steps and strategies on how to create online systems that will allow you to get new leads and customers online.

In this book, you will discover the website creation strategy that will allow you to generate leads and customers online, even while you sleep.

I teach you the in-depth process on how to create a website step by step that is geared toward getting customers online, recruits online, or both.

Traditional offline network marketing can be completely replaced with the methods you are about to learn.

Email marketing is the number one way to build relationships with prospects. Learn how collecting email addresses for a targeted audience will allow you to increase your online sales and customers.

Social media marketing is a great way to build trust and add value to your community. Many network markers don't realize how to use social media the right way and are spamming a lot of channels.

Learn how to use Facebook, Instagram, YouTube, Twitter, and Pinterest in a way that will allow you to generate endless leads online.

Find out how adding value and building an online community will make you more money rather than constantly promoting your company on social networks.

Learn how to make money with affiliate marketing and network marketing at the same time. Affiliate marketing is a great strategy that a lot of network marketers aren't using, but you should use it because not everyone will join your team, but they may purchase something that you recommend if you add enough value to their lives.

Use these proven strategies to increase your income online.

Make money online from more than just your network marketing company. Learn how creating automated systems online can bring you more money than your company.

Make money from those who won't ever join your team by diversifying your income.

Lastly, you will learn the skills that you need to focus on so you know that you're doing the right thing at all times when promoting your business online.

Learn the income producing activities for both network marketing and internet marketing so you'll always be focused, and have the ability to leverage your time.

The truth is, you can build a team and get customers both on and offline. Why not focus your efforts online so you'll be able to live a life of freedom.

This book will show you how to set up systems so that you will no longer have to trade time for money.

Don't wait any longer, don't be one of those network marketers who procrastinate because they're afraid of success. Take action right now and start reading this book.

Why I Wrote This Book

I wrote this book because I know how it is to struggle trying to build a team and get customers the traditional way. Although this did work, I started to realize that it wasn't for me.

I've always studied network marketing, so when I saw that many top leaders are building their teams exclusively online- I wanted a piece of the pie.

You know how I know that you can build your network marketing company online? Because there are network marketing companies that are exclusively online. No door to door, no vendor events, and the only way you'd be able to sign up is online.

With technology today, you're able to build a team worldwide and never have to deliver an order.

Although online cannot and will not ever replace the connection people have from meeting face to face, it still works and it's worth working toward.

After about a year of being in my company, I decided to go exclusively online and I saw how it is possible to do. That's why I wrote this book, to share with you non-traditional methods that can help grow your business online.

Because I know what it's like to deliver orders. I know what it's like to set up at a vendor show and no one buys from me. I know what it's like to have team meetings and no one show up. I've been there, and I want you to take action and start building your business online so you can set boundaries with your time, and have some freedom in your life.

Thanks again for reading *Internet Marketing For Network Marketers*, I hope you enjoy it!

Chapter 1: Website Creation Strategy

Creating a website is the first thing you'll need to do in order to take your business online. If you truly want to create a business that works 24/7, no matter if you're there are not, you will need a website.

Creating a website is actually quite simple, but it's the upkeep and consistency that will determine your success in the end.

Just like building a company offline, online will take work-- maybe, even more, work. But that's just in the beginning.

By setting up a website to bring you leads all day, you will be ahead of most people in the industry.

To get even further ahead, you will need to constantly add valuable content to your website which will, in turn, help build your team or get you more customers.

What Will Your Website Be About

As a network marketer, your website's subject will depend on what you're trying to do. Would you like to generate leads or customers?

You can always go back and create another website, but for now think about what you want to focus on.

The thing about success is you have to focus. What is the one thing that will bring you closer to your goal right now?

Is it having customers so you can have "right now money" and share the results which in turn will help to bring in more recruits?

Or is it bringing in more recruits, which in turn will define you as a leader and attract even more recruits?

Creating A Website To Get Customers

Building a website to generate customers will be simple but you need to know some basic things.

Do not use your company's name on your website. This is for two reasons: 1) it's most likely against your company's guidelines 2) You want to brand yourself in order to build trust with the leads that come in.

On this website, you'll be creating content that has to do with your company's products. For example, if your company sells shoes. You want to create pages that help people with making shoe selections, finding the right shoe, finding quality shoes, etc.

All your content on your website will be centered around one subject.

This is called a "niche site". A niche site is when you focus on one particular subject and create content around it.

If your content is valuable and helps the customer out, they will want to buy from you. This is when you can send them over to your company website where they'll make their purchases. More on this later.

Creating A Website To Get Recruits

Creating a site for recruits will be similar to creating a website for customers.

Again, make sure not to mention your company's name. You will be branding yourself.

Branding yourself is when you're using your name and not your company's name while providing value through your website content.

You don't want to mention your company's name because they are already branded. You want leads to join your team because of you.

Anyone can join a company, people will only stick around if they see you as a person that can help them get what they want.

You'll be creating content that helps other network markers. Think about the problems other network marketers just like you are having and solve them.

Once you do this you will create trust and be looked at as the "go to person" for network marketing.

In turn, they will either want to join your team or buy any information products and training you may have. More on information product creation later.

There is also an alternative for this if you truly want more targeted leads. You can create a website that is focused helping people in your particular company.

So when people search for more information about your company, you will have a site that has all the information they were looking for.

Leads will feel they have an advantage by joining your team because the content you've created for them is valuable and you look like you know what you're doing.

Why You Shouldn't Create A Website For Free

There are many sites out there like blogger.com and wordpress.com that allow you to set up an account and create a website for free.

I'm against these types of sites for many reasons.

The first reason is professionalism. Creating a website that ends with .wordpress or .blogger will look unprofessional.

People will take you and your business more seriously when you use a domain name that ends in .com

Also, if you go with those free sites you will not own your content. Whoever hosts your site will.

You also won't be able to monetize it the way you want to. Many of those sites have restrictions against things such as affiliate links and your own ads.

If you're not serious, and you're just dabbling in network marketing then you can create one of these websites. Just keep in mind that you will be giving up all control.

There are many benefits to using trustworthy hosting companies. You get customer support and you can create unlimited websites. This means you won't have to buy more hosting in order to create another site.

How To Create A Website

Now we're going to go into how to create an actual website. If you already own a website or blog you can move onto the next section.

Domain Name Rules

A domain name is the web address you type into a browser in order to get to a website. For example: Google.com is a domain name.

There are a few rules you need to follow when naming your website.

- Your domain name should have relevant keywords on what your site will be about

- Avoid using your company name

- Make sure to use .com

- Avoid using dashes

- Should be short and easy to remember

Registering A Domain Name

If you buy hosting first, sometimes you'll be able to get a free domain name with the host you choose.

I buy all my domain names from Godaddy because it allows for all of them to be in one place. You'll learn more about why you may want more than one domain name in later chapters.

Also, if you ever want to switch your hosting for any reason, you will not have to worry about transferring your domain name.

Transferring a domain name from one host to another can take up to three months.

To avoid all of this just register your domain name with Godaddy so if you ever want to change your host or use the domain name for something else you can easily just go in and do it.

Register you domain name in Godaddy by going to www.Godaddy.com and typing in the domain name you came up with of in the search box. Make sure to use the guidelines mentioned above.

If your first possible domain name is taken think of another one, keep trying until you find one that sounds right, looks right and works for you.

Make sure you buy a .com because this is the most universal ending for domain names and you will not encounter any trouble if using this.

Tip: To get the best price on your domain name search Google for "Godaddy Promo Codes"

Set Up Hosting

Next, you need to decide who you want to host your

website. There are many options to go with. There are a ton of hosts you can use.

Find out which is best for you, make sure first that the host offers a platform that you can easily set up WordPress.

I use a company called Bluehost. To buy hosting with them go to Bluehost.com. I recommend them because they have outstanding customer service and you can easily set up WordPress.

After finding a host, install WordPress and you're good to go.

***For a complete tutorial on how to set up your website visit www.networkmarketingkingdom.com/website ***

The Website Creation Strategy

Now that you've registered your domain, you've set up WordPress, you're ready to start creating content.

The content you create is what will constantly bring leads into your funnel so you can turn them into customers and recruits.

The goal here is to create content related to your particular product if you're trying to reach customers, or your knowledge of the industry if you're trying to get recruits.

Really find your niche. For example: If your product is related to makeup you can create a website with content about makeup tips, tutorials, product reviews, etc.

Avoid using your company name. Before you create any pages make sure you use Google Keywords Tool to find keywords to use in your pages that are not too high in competition and now too low.

There are also paid tools that can help with your keyword research and find keywords that people are searching for. This may be worth it if you want to do in-depth research or find keywords and competition.

This will allow your site to rank in Google. Use search engine optimization (SEO) to get found for different words and phrases so you can drive traffic to your site.

My favorite WordPress plugin to use for this is WordPress SEO Yoast. SEO Yoast shows you how to optimize your pages and posts for the search engines.

As you can see, internet marketing is a huge learning curve. There is so much to learn, it is a lot of work.

Your website's keywords is only one way you will get traffic to your website, though. You will also get traffic from email and social media marketing. More on that later.

Traffic is very important. There are tons of ways to get traffic and you want to expose your site to as many people possible.

The equation is simple. More traffic=More leads.

The thing that will make you successful at creating a website that stands out is you have to create content for a very targeted audience. The content you create has to teach someone how to do something.

When teaching others how to do something, make sure if they follow your blueprint that they'll get results.

After getting results from using your free content, they'll become raving fans and buy any product or service you have to offer in the future.

Raise your standards when it comes to creating your content. Do the research that is necessary and don't be lazy about it.

If you truly put your all into your website, you will stick out from all the other marketers trying to do the exact same thing. In turn, people will become attracted to you because you will be known as an expert in whatever you're teaching about.

The websites that do best are the ones that teach someone how to do something.

Keep in mind that you can easily create more than one website. If you use a host that allows you to have unlimited domains, you can create lots of websites and only pay for hosting once a year. To create a new site all you'd have to do is buy a new domain name.

So you'll be able to create sites for recruiting, getting customers, and possibly one for your team.

As long as your creating lots of content that is valuable and use the proper keywords, you will generate traffic.

You may be wondering why I don't suggest you create a blog. This is because a blog will constantly have to be updated.

You want a static website that allows you to create something once and leave everything else up to the automated system.

So make sure the content you create is evergreen and not about events or subjects that are time dependent. If you create content that is not evergreen you can use it in your social media updates.

Creating A Team Site

Creating a team site is the best way to leverage your time. If you put out valuable content on another website or through other channels such as social media or email then people will want to join your team.

People will also want to join your team once they see your professionalism you have by having a dedicated team site. The best way to get more team members is to get results and share results. In turn, this will attract others and they'll want to do what you're doing.

Make your team site a membership site exclusive only to your team members. Here you can walk them step-by-step through the process after they sign up to join your team.

You can also offer them training and everything they need to be successful on your team.

This will allow you to leverage your time. You will not have to answer the same questions over and over again. If you put everything you would say to a new team member on that site, you will save them time and you time.

Chapter 2: Email Marketing

Email marketing is the way you will capture leads that visit your website or squeeze page. It's also a way that to get traffic back to your website.

To capture the names and emails of your prospects you will need email software. The most popular is Aweber, this is what I use.

Once you buy the software you can place an opt-in box on your website so that visitors can enter their name and email.

The leads you collect from your website are yours to keep no matter what happens. If something happens to your website-- you'll always have your list to refer back to.

This is the importance of creating a list. A list can also be profitable and can allow you to send emails without having to actively type them out each time you want to send one out.

This is where the automated system comes in. In Aweber you can create a series of follow-up messages that will go out to your email list. You can schedule them to go out whenever you want.

These email autoresponders will take you out of the equation so you can work on other things that are income producing activities-- like making phone calls to leads about your company, showing leads your presentation, and following up.

Or, if you ever decide to take your business online, you can live a freedom lifestyle where you have systems set up that you're earning from so you can live the life you want.

You will also have leads calling you about your company instead of having to call them.

Set up and send out autoresponders messages that help your target audience, bring them back to your website, and puts them in a position to want to buy what you're selling or join your team.

Set up about 10 autoresponders to start off with. Send them out about every other day.

How To Get Leads To Opt In

People are not going to just come to your website and enter their email address and name unless you're offering them something of value.

Keep in mind that your audience is most likely already getting tons of emails a day and they do not want any more spam coming into their inbox.

So make sure the messages you send out are quality and helpful.

Types Of Emails You May Send To Your List:

- new blog post

- new product

- new podcast episode

- sale on a product

- new video

- free product

- etc.

Always have a good reason to email your list, if you have something of value to share, send them an email.

Create an opt-in offer to get leads on your list

An opt-in offer is something you create that you give your visitors for free that will make them want to get on your email list.

Make your opt-in offer something relevant to what your target audience will want.

Some ideas: Free course, eBook, guide, free report, audio, conference call, interview with an expert, free consultation...

Whatever you decide to give away will be digital. Try to make it something that is independent of your time so that you don't have to be there to deliver it.

After your offer is created, get the link to it and put it in the first autoresponder message that is sent immediately when a lead opts-in.

This allows you to give them something of value for free without having to be there. Which in turn builds trust and likeability.

The follow-up messages you create after that should be related to your target audience and the information on your website.

Create a new email list when necessary. A new list is necessary if you want to create an audience for another website you have, or when you want to target a different audience.

By creating an email list you, in turn, will get traffic back to your website or straight back to your company website so leads can either buy from you or join your team. All of this will be on autopilot.

Broadcast messages

Most email software allows you to send out broadcast messages to your list.

Above we talked about autoresponders, but a broadcast message may be necessary depending on the message you're sending out.

For example, if you have a sale on your product or a special offer that is only for a limited time, you want to send out a broadcast message.

If you're worried about people getting more than one email from you in a day, make sure to schedule your autoresponders on certain days so you can send broadcast messages on particular days.

This may not be automated, but it's a great way to keep your list updated on new information such as events, sales, and promotions.

The Takeaway

Email marketing will be the way you make most of your money through online marketing overall. People check their email daily, and for a lot of people it's what they do as soon as they wake up in the morning.

Keep in mind that there's a lot of competition out there so treat your list like gold. Only send them emails that will further their business or save them some money.

Make sure to always keep a backup of your list. It's your biggest asset. If you haven't started email marketing and you want to build your network marketing business online-- the best time to get started building a list was yesterday.

If you don't learn anything from this book, learn that email marketing is the way of the future. And it can be the difference between becoming a top earner or losing everything you've worked to build online.

I have a **free video** on how to get started with email marketing. You can check it out by visiting:

http://www.argenaolivis.com/email-marketing-101/

In this training, I walk you through how to set up your opt-in offer and create autoresponder messages.

Chapter 3: Social Media Marketing

Social media marketing is another way that you can generate leads and customers online. It's also a way to get traffic back to your website or squeeze page/email list.

I'm going to go over the most popular social media sites: Facebook, Instagram, Twitter, Pinterest, and YouTube.

Make sure that you're only focusing on one or two social media sites at a time. It's okay to create profiles for each site, but make sure you're only giving your attention to one or two.

I say this because you want to master one form of social media before moving on to the next. Building your business online will take extreme focus and consistency.

Make sure to measure your results. If you see you're getting more results from one site, then focus on that one site. Don't spread yourself too thin. **Learn everything you can about one of these social media channels and give it all you've got.**

Facebook

Facebook is a way for you to market your business. Use Facebook to get leads online. Create a Facebook Fan Page.

Share quality tips and content with your Facebook fans. Facebook is a way to build a community of trusted and loyal fans.

Use Facebook to get more email subscribers. Tell your fans about the email offer you've created in order to get them on your list. You can post about your opt-in offer and create a page app for it (page apps are only seen by desktop users).

Share tips and content that you've written on your website, new videos, new podcasts, webinars, conference calls, etc. Also, share any news and events you have and promotions your company may be having.

Share Results

Sharing results will allow you to inspire others and ultimately strike curiosity about what exactly you're doing.

Make sure to post when a new team member joins your team. Have their picture and also, tag them in the post. This will make the team member feel special and also make you look like an authority.

Share when you get a big bonus or when something amazing happens. Whenever you get extraordinary monetary rewards from your company share it on your fan page. This shows your hard work and it also inspires others.

It lets other see what's possible. It also makes you look like you know what you're doing. And if you look like you know what you're doing, people will think you can help them to achieve the same results.

Don't just post about your company or product. People love to see things like lifestyle images and really get to know you.

Connect on a deeper level with your fans. Ask questions and share resources with them that have been helpful to you.

Update your page about 8-10 times a day. Preferably

once every hour.

To automate this, you can use a tool like Hootsuite. Or you can schedule posts directly from your Facebook page because Facebook has a scheduler.

Instagram

Instagram is a great way to capture leads. Use hashtags a lot. Here are my favorites:

#entrepreneur #internetmarketing #business #personaldevelopment #mlm #networkmarketing

Instagram is an app where you can share images or very short videos. Use images of your lifestyle and take screen shots of things you're working on.

Also, similar to Facebook make sure to post your results.

You can use apps to create images and share tips or quotes. My favorite apps to use for Instagram are word swag, textgram, or aviary.

Use whatever hashtags are relevant to your topic or to your particular post.

If you use a lot of great hashtags you won't have any problems getting followers and leads. You can direct message on Instagram too-- a lot of people don't know that.

Make sure you make the descriptions under your images enticing. Use emojis and different symbols to stand out.

I don't know about you but I hate typing long descriptions directly from my phone, so I usually type the descriptions from my desktop and send it to myself via email. After that, I copy and paste the description into Instagram. I do the same for my hashtags.

Make sure you use screen shots when you want to showcase a product or service you offer. Screenshots are an easy way to show prospects what you're talking about.

You can schedule your Instagram posts by using postso.com to automate this. Instagram iss the most difficult social media site to automate.

Twitter

Twitter is a great way to find out what people in the industry are up to because you can search for a specific phrase and see what people are posting in real time.

With Twitter, you can share simple tips and links because you are only alloted up to 140 characters per post.

You are able to call attention to others by using their twitter name in your posts.

It's also a great way to get a lot of exposure. You can do this by using hashtags for things that are trending.

The best way to automate your twitter is to link it to your Facebook page so that every time you post on Facebook the same post will appear in your Twitter feed.

If you're focusing more on Facebook this is a great way to automate things. But if you want to focus on Twitter, post to twitter individually from Facebook.

There are also schedulers you can use such as buffer app and HootSuite. But if you want to automate, it's best to schedule your posts on Facebook and have your post on Facebook show up in your Twitter feed.

Just like Instagram, make sure to use relevant hashtags in your tweets.

Pinterest

Pinterest can be an amazing traffic source to your website.

Pinterest is a social media site that is similar to Instagram because it's image based.

So just like Instagram, make sure to post relevant pictures.

Some ideas include:

- screen shots of a new blog post

- quote images

- screen shots of projects you're working on

- screen shots of your information products

- screenshots of the products your company sells

- lifestyle images

The great thing about Pinterest is you can add videos. So when you make YouTube videos make sure to post them on Pinterest.

Some great free resources to make images are www.picmonkey.com and www.canva.com

Don't forget to use hashtags on Pinterest too! These will allow your images to be found and repinned.

Pinterest has an audience of mainly women, and if you sell anything women can use--this can definitely be a source of traffic to you.

Make sure that you put a pin its button on the images on your website to make it easy for people to share.

Remember, more traffic=more leads.

You can use a tool such as www.curalate.com to automate your pins. Pinterest, like Instagram, is more difficult to automate.

YouTube

YouTube is one of the best channels to build trust with your audience and in turn, generate more leads online.

The thing about video is not everyone does it. Many people are afraid of what they will look like on camera or let things like not having a professional camera stop them.

If you post videos you will already be ahead of those who are too afraid to.

And keep in mind that you don't have to be in your videos. You can create training using PowerPoint presentations and record your computer screen and upload it as a video.

To record your screen, you can use free software like Jing or Screen-Cast-O-Matic.

Video marketing is amazing and if you haven't, you should start making videos.

Videos can be time-consuming though, but there is a way to get around this and be more productive.

It's called video batching. What you do is create a list of topics for videos you want to create and record all the videos in one sitting. To come up with topics, use a something like Google AdWords Keywords Tool.

You can batch videos for the week or for the month depending on how often you want to post.

You can also turn this into an income stream by signing up for Youtube's partner program. This is where Google Adsense pays you a portion of what they are making from advertisements.

You can create a video and a blog post on the same topic and embed the video into your blog post, this will give your visitors the ultimate experience. The best way to save time and get the most out of this is to record your video and have it transcribed.

You can have your video transcribed for cheap by using outsourcing services such as Fiverr.com.

The visitors that love to watch video will be able to do so, and the ones who like to read will do so-- it's a win-win.

Another great thing about this is the ability to turn the audio from your YouTube video into a podcast.

Here's how it goes: video > audio/podcast> transcription/blog post> lead generation from multiple sources.

You will also be more easily found in the search engine if you use keywords that are being searched for and are not too competitive.

You can use programs like Windows Live Movie Maker to edit your videos. And you can go to Fiverr.com to get an intro. It all depends on how much time and effort you're willing to put into it.

As long as you have good lighting and sound, viewers will watch your videos if they are into what you are teaching or showing.

To save time, create a document of all the information you want to put in your video description. When you upload your videos in the future, copy and paste the document into your YouTube description.

Make sure to include a link back to your website. Mention your opt-in offer in order to get more people on your email list. Preferably have a link to your squeeze page as the first item in your description.

To automate this, YouTube has a scheduler inside of it that will post your videos for whatever time you want them released.

As you can see, video is a game changer, and can be critical to your success.

Keep in mind that YouTube is the second biggest search engine in the world, so you may want to get on there.

Chapter 4: Affiliate Marketing

Don't have your own training products yet? That's, fine. You don't need your own product to make extra income online.

You can make an extra stream of income in addition to your company by affiliate marketing.

Affiliate marketing is when you earn a commission on a product by someone clicking on a unique link provided to you by the owner of the product and buying the product through your unique link.

When you promote a product make sure it's relevant to your audience. Keep in mind that although you're an independent distributor through your company-- some of what you're doing may be similar to affiliate marketing because you are sending people to your online store so they can buy through you-- it's not much different.

But everyone may not be interested in buying your company's products or training. So if you feel that your audience (such as your email list) can truly benefit from a product, become an affiliate for it and recommend it to your audience.

In order to get people to buy through your affiliate link, you need to give them a reason. Tell them the benefits of the product or demonstrate how to use the product.

Do not recommend products that you haven't used yourself, if you do you won't be able to give an honest review of it.

It would be better if you could make a video demonstrating the product so people can see you, and see that you actually own it.

Some tricks for getting more affiliate sales:

- create bonuses for the people that buy through your link

- Buy domain names and set them up so they'll forward straight to the affiliate offer

- Give an honest review, no product is perfect so let them know what it lacked

Try to develop a relationship with the affiliate. They may do a special offer for your audience.

Many affiliates will give you email swipes and other tools to be successful. Take their advice and see what works best for promoting their offers.

Make sure to create an affiliate disclaimer/disclosure policy on your website. (FTC Disclaimer).

Do not try to sell too early and make sure what you're trying to sell is relevant to your audience.

Clickbank is the best place to find offers to promote. But there are tons of other channels like commission junction and share-a-sale.

The best way to find out if a company has an affiliate program is searching the company's name in Google and putting the words "affiliate program" at the end.

You can also check by going directly to their website and scrolling down to the bottom to see if they have a link for affiliates.

All in all, affiliate marketing done right is a way to make some extra money online in addition to your network marketing company.

Chapter 5: Diversify Your Income Online

Now that you are getting some income from selling your products online and getting residual income from the recruits you've brought on-- it's time to diversify your income.

You always want to have multiple streams of income coming in, just to be safe and also to make more money.

Keep in mind that you don't own your company and they can make changes at any time-- this can really influence your income.

So to avoid putting all your eggs in one basket, you may want to create other streams of income online.

Don't try to get into too many things too soon, though. You can work on things on a quarterly basis. You'll get the best results when you focus on one project at a time. So make sure you meet your income goal with one project before moving on to another.

Ads

If your website is getting at least 25+ visitors a day, consider putting up advertising.

I say wait until you get 25+ unique visitors a day because there is no point of applying for advertising if you don't have any traffic because you won't make any money.

The most popular ones are Google AdSense, Infolinks, and Media.net

You place ads on your site and when a visitor clicks on them you get paid a percentage.

Make sure to never click on your own ads and don't tell anyone else to click them for you. Many of these programs are very strict and if you're not careful they can ban you for life.

Never make ads your only source of income. It's too risky.

Information Products

Another way to diversify your income is to create your own information products.

Information products are things like eBooks, audios, video courses (Udemy), etc.

Anything that can be created and sent out digitally is an information product.

Depending on how long you've been in network marketing you may already have some products you can put up for sale on your site.

You can sell audio like conference call recordings and team training.

You can also sell seats to webinars.

If you're more focused on getting customers rather than team building, then you may want to consider creating an eBook around a the product you sell.

You can also put your eBook up on Kindle and make an income while still directing traffic to your website and growing your email list. Click here to get my free kindle book creation course.

You can consider creating a membership site or group that people have to pay to use. It could include network marketing training.

There are tons of products you can create, you just have to think big and take action. The money is there-- you just have to have invest in your knowledge and share what you know works.

You do not have to be an expert to provide value. No information is really new, it's all recycled. But people may connect with you better or they may like the way you teach better than others.

Take what you've been learning and share it with the world. And turn your ideas into profit.

All in all, make sure that if you create a product that everything is automated. Don't create physical products if you truly want to work smarter.

Keep in mind that you will still have to work hard at first even if everything is automated. It takes consistency and motivation to get things set up and running smoothly.

But it's totally worth it, right?

Your product should be created once and independent of your time if you want to create passive income.

If you really want to expand your reach, put your digital product on Clickbank to reach more people. Others will become an affiliate for it and a help you to sell it.

A customer should be able to purchase your product and pay for it and the money should be automatically sent to your bank account so you won't have to be there to for the transaction.

This process is easy to set up with programs like Ejunkie, Gumroad, and PayPal.

Chapter 6: Skills To Work On

Internet marketing and network marketing are both steep learning curves. Trying to learn both can be overwhelming.

Here are the skills you will need in order to succeed in both.

Personal Development

Personal development is the number one skill you need to focus on. Your mindset is truly important.

The person who is motivated and ready to work will always beat the person who is not sure of themselves or their possibilities.

If you procrastinate and don't take action, it's because of your mindset. As you learn new things and try to have a better life there will be many obstacles that come in your way.

Becoming a better person, in general, will increase your income dramatically.

So make sure you focus on staying motivated and working on your mindset.

Check out my book Network Marketing Mindset for encouragement and confidence building.

Adding Value

You're most likely in network marketing for one main reason-- to make more money. And there's nothing wrong with that.

But what you have to realize is you're truly going to have

to have something of value to offer people if you want to make money online.

The more valuable you are, the more money you will make. When creating free information try not to hold anything back and really blow people away.

There is so much free information out there that you shouldn't be trying to keep secrets because someone somewhere is helping people get results by sharing everything they know and more.

If you have a product and you don't want to share everything out of respect for the people that have already paid for it. That's understandable. But make sure to try your best to help people get results with the free information you put out there.

Today there are millions of websites and products-- you have to be different.

They say that the amount of money you make is a direct correlation to how much value you create. So if you're not making any money, you should take a step back and see what you can improve on.

Don't hold anything back. **Be obsessed with your customers** and don't worry about competition. If you are consistent and truly want to help others then you're already ahead.

Invest in yourself. Then after you learn something and get results from it-- teach it in your own way.

Copy Writing

This is a high paid skill that many people don't think to pursue and learn.

If you want to sell online, you're going to have to have a

way with words.

This skill will come in handy with sales letters, descriptions, and emails.

SEO

Search engine optimization is another skill you may want to learn. Although there are plugins like SEO Yoast that help you, you still want to know how to use keywords so you can rank in the search engines.

You may be consistent at creating content, but it's useless if no one sees it.

Content Syndication

Work smarter. Learn to re-purpose your content.

For example: Create a blog post on how to lose weight >create a video on how to lose weight > put that video on Youtube> embed that video into your blog post> tell others about your new blog post on Social media> Send that blog post to your email ist

Here are other ways to re-purpose and syndicate content:

- Turn YouTube videos into audios and podcasts

- Turn a collection of blog posts into an eBook

- Turn blog posts into a power point presentation and put on Slideshare

- Turn videos into blog posts

- Use all the content from your website and turn it into a book

- Take a screen shot of your blog post and post on

social media

There are many ways you can use your content to create other content.

Tracking Performance

Use tools such as Google Analytics and Statcounter to track your performance.

These tools will tell you where your traffic is coming from and what keywords are getting the most attention.

Also, create a spreadsheet in excel and track your social media engagement, affiliate sells, and other income over time.

See what's working and what's not working. Focus more on what's working and leave the other stuff behind.

Traffic

Learn the different sources where you can get traffic online. Focus on the top two things that are bringing you the most traffic.

Master your traffic sources and then move on to other sources to expand your reach.

Here is how it goes:
traffic>leads>conversions>sales>happy customer>shared experience>referrals> traffic

The Takeaway

If you want to truly maximize your business and profits, when your business starts to grow and you're making a sizeable income. It may be time to hire a virtual assistant that can help you with a lot of these tasks.

It's a lot of work to create and syndicate content. You're

going to need help or you'll be working in your business, not on your business.

In time, you'll want to hire a team to handle customer service, social media updates, etc.

In the meantime, if you have the money outsource what you can be using services such as Fiverr.com and Odesk.com. There your can find someone to work for you for an affordable price.

I know that you have what it takes to be a successful internet network marketer. There's a lot of competition, but no one can replace you. Not everyone is working smart. And not everyone had the right mindset to keep pushing even when times get hard.

Good luck on your journey to development as a better person and a better marketer.

Conclusion

Thank you again for reading this book!

I hope this book was able to help you to discover how to generate leads online.

The next step is to take action!

Finally, if you enjoyed Internet Marketing for Network Marketers, then I'd like to ask you for a favor, would you be kind enough to leave a review for this book on Amazon? It'd be greatly appreciated!

By reviewing this book, you'll give me feedback on what I can do better or if I've done a great job. It also helps others to find the book.

Thank you and good luck with everything!

Network Marketing Mindset

Personal Development and Confidence Building for Network Marketers

www.networkmarketingkingdom.com

Table of Contents

Bonus Video: How To Get Leads and Customers Online

Subscribe To Get Free Tips On How To Generate Leads and Get Customers

When you subscribe to get network marketing tips via email, you will get free access to exclusive subscriber-only resources. All you have to do is enter your email address to the right to get instant access.

These resources will help you get more out of your business – to be able to reach your goals, have more motivation, be at your best, and live the life you've always dreamed of. I'm always adding new resources, which you will be notified of as a subscriber. These will help you get an endless amount of leads and customers.

**Visit
www.networkmarketingkingdom.com/video
to Access The Bonus Video**

Introduction

I want to thank you and congratulate you for reading the book, *"Network Marketing Mindset: Personal Development and Confidence Building for Network Marketers"*.

This book contains proven steps and strategies on how to deal with the daily rejection in the network marketing profession.

Network marketing is by far the most difficult industry to learn and stay encouraged in.

Many people quit because they don't have the leadership skills and confidence to stick it out.

Daily rejection from recruits and leads can be very destructive to your confidence.

It's nice to say "so what, who's next" when people hurt your feelings. Trying to recruit can cause a lot of difficulties when it comes to friendships and relationships.

If you don't learn the right skills, it's possible that you can alienate people to the point where they don't want to be around you, because they think you're going to try and recruit them.

Network marketing itself has a bad rep to a lot of people not in the industry, they may think the opportunity you're offering them is a pyramid scheme or a scam.

If you're working the business, this constant rejection can take a lot out of you. It will leave you wondering if it's the right thing for you.

In this book, I will go into why network marketing isn't for everyone and ways you can have leads come to you instead of you chasing them.

Also, how to become a better person overall. How to live a better and more fulfilled life.

How to never give up on your dreams of financial freedom and continue on your journey to network marketing success.

Let's be honest-- network marketing is a people business. You're going to get your feelings involved.

This business is built on not just your effort, but the effort your team puts in.

That's why you constantly have to focus on making yourself a better person. Like attracts like.

So if you become more confident and get your mindset right you and your team will become unstoppable.

With these simple strategies, you will learn how to make this your best business and your best life.

Thanks again for reading *Network Marketing Mindset*, I hope you enjoy it!

Chapter 1: Believe In Yourself and Your Business

Believing in yourself sounds easy, but it's one of the hardest things to do. This is because today there is so much competition and it seems like you'll never get a piece of the pie.

But what you have to realize is, there's always going to be someone better than you at something.

Don't ever waste your time trying to compare yourself to others. It's okay to model them in order to strive for what they have, but it's never okay to compare yourself.

You don't know what it took to achieve what they have. Maybe they have more time than you, maybe they don't have any kids, maybe they work 15 hour days, you just never know.

Don't compare their situation to yours. You also don't know how long they've been doing what they're doing.

When you look at successful network marketers, you don't see the late nights, the studying, and skill building it took for them to get to where they are.

They may have poured hundreds and thousands of dollars into their education. You just don't know-- so don't compare.

To believe in yourself you have to learn to stop comparing yourself and start working on yourself.

You can start by asking yourself the most important question: "Is network marketing right for me?"

Network marketing does have a ton of benefits but

realize that it's a people business and you have to depend on people in order to make money.

Also, realize you don't have a lot of control of your business, your company can change the compensation plan at any time.

But one thing does remain the same, you can earn as much as you want. There is not a cap. Also, the startup cost is low, and you gain confidence by interacting with others.

There are many pros and cons, but are you down for whatever is yet to come? Are you willing to deal with people quitting and your company changing its policies?

If so, you believe in your business and the business model.

If you can get past the negatives you can move forward.

Do you believe in yourself? Do you believe you have what it takes to be successful in life?

If not, what's holding you back?

If you're reading this book you need encouragement. Daily!

Start taking your mindset seriously. Do what it takes to start thinking and acting like someone of value.

You can start believing in yourself by accomplishing something. Set a goal to recruit at least one person by next week.

If you achieve this goal, your belief will skyrocket.

But you need more than a goal, you need a plan.

Start investing in books and courses about network

marketing. Take yourself seriously and your business seriously.

Once you learn the skills your confidence will increase.

Get yourself organized. Stop playing games, and get out there and do the best you can with what you have!

Don't let anyone tell you that you're not good enough. Ignore the people who tell you that this business isn't worth doing.

Ignore the people who aren't on the same track as you. It's time to let go of some of those relationships that are dragging you down. And you know which ones I'm talking about.

You're only as good as you feel. Start taking better care of your body.

Be the best you. Wake up early and go to sleep late.

Having success is going to take sacrifice.

This means no T.V. (especially the news), no video games, no senseless spending, no vacations.

If you truly want to reach your goals, give up some of the things that are wasting your time.

Become more of a productive person.

Start saying yes to the things that will make you a better person. Like seminars, working out, and eating healthy.

Get out of your comfort zone and start being more serious and disciplined.

Chapter 2: How To Stay Motivated

One of the hardest things to do in any business is to stay motivated. Although we want to go full time and quit our jobs, we often time lack the discipline to do so.

The great thing about this is we do want more. We know we have a way to go full time if we work hard and stay committed.

But getting there is the struggle. To wake up every morning ready to work is not normal, as human beings, we have mental blocks that at times hold us back from success.

We want to be better and reach our full potential. We want to make that last phone call to that prospect. And we definitely want to be the best upline in the world, but we fall short mainly because of our beliefs.

Many times we don't take action because we don't know what we should be doing.

Daily Routine

In order to stay motivated, you need a daily routine. This is something that you will do NO MATTER WHAT. This is the thing that will allow you to plant seeds that will grow and come back to you for years to come.

The first thing to do is decide how many hours a day you want to work your business. Keep in mind that this is something you will be doing every single day with no days off.

I think three hours a day is a reasonable amount for

anyone. Rather your full time or part time you can squeeze in three hours a day to build your business.

Of course, you can adjust it to make it more hours, but the thing we are going to practice here is consistency.

Your daily routine should be something that you do every day to grow your business and should include income producing activities.

To create your daily routine, find what income producing activities you need to do every day to grow your business.

Once you've found them write them on a piece of paper. Then you need to separate these activities into timed tasks.

For example: Follow-up with prospects (1 hour)

However, many hours you gave yourself (remember 3 or more hours) for your daily routine, make sure all your income producing activities will get done in the allotted time.

Income Producing Activities

If you're not focused on income producing activities, it can lower your motivation because you won't be seeing any results.

Also, knowing that you're working on income producing activities daily will increase your confidence.

The income producing activities in network marketing are:

- Showing your presentation to as many prospects as possible

- Talking to people about your opportunity

- Following up with leads

- Training your team to show presentation, talk people about the opportunity, and to follow up

So if you want to create a daily routine, these activities should be included in them.

Example:

Daily Routine (every day): 3 hours
-30 min show presentation to 2 people
-30min talk to 5 people about my opportunity
-1 hour follow up with leads
-1-hour team training

Whatever works best for you and your schedule, and of course you can up a number of hours and time spent on these different tasks.

Setting Goals

Goal setting is another way to stay motivated. Have you ever heard of SMART goals?

S- Specific
M- Measurable
A- Achievable
R-Relevant & Realistic
T- Time Bound

This is a checklist that you can use to make sure you're setting goals.

Having goals allows you to feel refreshed and motivated each month. Monthly goals work best to stay motivated.

Make sure your goals are not result oriented, so you won't get depressed. What I mean by that is make sure they don't focus on results because if you don't get that result, you'll feel like you failed.

Focus on action steps that you can take to achieve your goals instead.

For example, instead of setting a goal to recruit 10 people in a month. Set a goal to reach out to 10 people a day.

Your consistent effort with income producing activities will bring you results. There is no need to put yourself in a situation where you can't control the outcome.

Network marketing is based on people, you can't control any outcome. You cannot control what people do. You also cannot control what changes your company makes.

Therefore, a SMART Goal for your business might be: I will easily show my presentation to 60 people by 00/00/00 <== enter date here).

Have at least 3 goals for the month and make sure to keep them in plain sight. You can use things like a big white board or a note by your computer. Make sure to read them every day to stay motivated and focused.

Envision The Life You Want

You may lack motivation because you're not sure what type of lifestyle you want to live. What type of lifestyle would make your life must fulfilled and happy?

Start by doing an exercise where you close your eyes and envision how you truly want your life to be. From the time you wake up and the time you go to sleep.

If time and money were not a problem, what would you do with your day?

Be very specific. What type of car do you want to drive,

what would your house look like? What would you do with your family?

Write down your dream life. Keep this close and refer back to it whenever you need a pick me up.

If you really want to speed things up, read this when you wake up and before you go to bed.

Your Why

Knowing why you do what you do will help you to get out of bed in the morning and get to work.

If you know your purpose for living, and you are sure of everything you're working towards-- then you're well on your way to financial freedom.

Is your why to help others start their own business? Helping others to start their own business can be a life changer. Even if they don't stick with network marketing and decide to go in a different direction, think of the impact it can have on their life.

You offering them an opportunity to see that they can run a business may help them realize that there's a better life for them and that they have what it takes to be successful.

Accountability Partner

Find an accountability partner that you can work with weekly to discuss your progress and your goals.

Hold each other accountable for everything you're working toward. Your accountability partner should be someone who is like-minded and motivated like you.

They don't have to be in network marketing, but they should be an entrepreneur so you two can relate.

Mastermind

Join a mastermind group for network marketing. This is a place to share your ideas and progress with others.

This will keep you motivated and inspired when you see others getting results.

There are many free groups on Facebook and others that cost. Find one that's right for you and that you'll benefit from.

Make sure not to just read what's in the group but to stay active and participate.

If you can't' seem to find one that's right for you, start your own.

Events

Events are always a motivator. They make you get your off your butt and into the mood to take action right away.

Events work so well because you get exposed to the many people who are doing well-- that means this is possible for you.

It makes you want to be the next one on stage. Therefore, you take massive action!

Attend network marketing events, your company events and meetings, business seminars, etc.

Commitment

To stay motivated in your company, you have to be committed. This means doing things even when you don't feel like it.

This means taking action even when you're uncomfortable.

Commitment means staying up until it's finished, not going to sleep when you're tired.

It means answering your team members call for the 3rd time in the row that day.

It means being a person of your word and following up.

Make a decision today to be committed to your goals and your dreams and motivation won't be a factor.

Habits

Develop habits that other successful network marketers have. Habits go right along with discipline.

By creating habits, you'll find yourself doing what you need to do without having to fight with procrastination.

You'll start to do things without having to think twice; to the point where if you don't do it, you won't feel right.

The best way to develop a habit is to start off small. For example: Challenge yourself to wake up at 5am every single day. As you create these small habits, they will turn into big successes.

Research shows that you shouldn't try to form more than three habits at one time. So pick three small habits right now that you want to start implementing starting tomorrow. Tell yourself that you'll stick with them for at least a month.

Chapter 3: How To Deal With Rejection

Rejection is something that is going to happen in this business. You cannot escape it, you will hear the word "no", or even worse.

You may sometimes ask yourself if it's worth it, well... that's for you to decide. If your ultimate goal is financial freedom, there are many business models that are more rejection free.

But I'm assuming since you've purchased this book that you're in network marketing for more than the business model-- it's because you want more than money.

You want others to see you successful, you want to build confidence, you want to meet like-minded people, and you want to change people lives.

You chose to do this. Everything you wake up and do is a choice and an investment.

People are going to be rude, they are going to laugh at you, and they are going to tell you that you can't make money doing this.

Let their disbelief be the reason that you make it to the top! Do not allow people to decide rather or not you will be successful.

Use that as fuel to make tons of money and have fun doing it.

But the truth is you'll never truly get over being rejected, it's something you deal with.

Rejection will make you stronger, and it can either make you or break you.

If you use rejection as fuel you will make it. If you use it and let it get to you – you will end up giving up.

If you ever leave the network marketing profession, do it on your own terms, not because of something someone said.

It's natural for people to be skeptical about things they have no idea about. Also, you don't know their story-- and this profession isn't right for everyone.

Just be yourself and reach out. You're giving them an opportunity to better their lives-- they can take it or leave it.

It's not you that they don't trust, it's the business or business in general.

Many people are afraid, and it takes a few exposures for people to really feel that this may be something they want to commit to.

Try first to build trust and rapport with leads instead of telling them to just join your team or buy from you.

Remember that it's all about the numbers. Many will join you, many will leave you, but it's only a few you need to gain success.

Don't be afraid to ask, and don't be afraid to get rejected.

This is why I recommend daily motivation and daily action. Make sure your mind is right before you talk to anyone.

Your mindset is what determines your earning potential. Feed your mind what it needs daily and you will do what you have to.

You only live once, so decide now to live a fearless life of freedom.

And make sure to do something, keep busy. The more you think, the less you'll make. If you find yourself thinking too much, you may get depressed. Your mind is a tricky thing that wants you to remain comfortable.

Implement things right away, stay busy, and only fill your mind with positive things.

Chapter 4: How To Have Confidence and Attract People

Confidence is not something you're born with. It's something you must work on every day-- just like motivation.

Confidence building is not simple and it takes dedication and a "can do" attitude.

If your "why" is big enough, and you have goals set for yourself; your confidence levels should have already increased.

We are confident in the things we know work. So if you're constantly putting in the work by being committed to your daily routine then you are well on your way.

Confidence comes from within but the way we feel and look physically can also play a huge role.

Encouragement

Gain confidence through encouragement and support of other network marketers and team members.

Also, remember that your team members need encouragement and recognition constantly in order to feel appreciated.

Keep yourself around encouraging people that are want to see you make it.

Read personal development books and quotes that uplift your spirit.

Do your best to stay encouraged and watch your

confidence soar.

Health

You only feel as good as you look. Take great care of yourself. We all know the things we should do, but taking care of our health can be a struggle sometimes.

It takes dedication and will power to truly become healthy.

But what is your health worth to you? When you do better you feel better.

This means exercise, eating right, and drinking plenty of water.

Your health is an investment. What's the point of making all this money in network marketing if you won't be around to enjoy it?

Style

Everyone has their own style. The way you dress may be increasing or decreasing your confidence.

Believe me, I'd rather make a million bucks than look like a million bucks-- but you look how you feel.

What can you wear that will make you feel more confident in yourself?

If you don't own it, maybe it's time you invest in yourself.

Attraction Marketing

I don't know if you've ever heard, but attraction marketing is the new way of network marketing.

This is when you're not asking people to join your team, but people are coming to you.

This is when people are calling you and buying from you because something about you that they're at attracted to.

To succeed at attraction marketing you have to be the "go to person" in your company or in the network marketing industry in general.

Once people see you as an expert, they will be attracted to you and want to join your team.

To be the go-to person, make sure that the material you learn you share with others.

No one is born an expert, we all had to learn from someone.

Really start studying network marketing and be a wealth of knowledge and share what you know.

This is what attraction marketing is all about. Wanting to be that person or be near that person because of the value you've provided for them.

When you help someone or you seem to be the go-to person-- everyone will swing your way.

Chapter 5: Vision Board and Affirmations

These two strategies are ones that will allow you to have a more productive and positive mindset, which in turn will allow you to bring success into your life.

Vision Board

A vision board is a board that is dedicated to what you want to see your life look like in the future.

All you have to do is get a poster board, magazines, tape, and scissors.

Get magazines that are geared toward what you want your life to be like.

The best ones are travel magazines.

Cut out words and pictures of things you want to come into your life.

The idea here is to envision what you want your life to be like. This is an opportunity for you to learn more about yourself.

Below is a picture of my vision board for this year, just to give you some ideas.

You can have all images or all words, it's up to you. Just

make it your own and make it true to your heart.

Merge your goals and the vision for your life into your vision board and you're good to go.

Hang this in a place where you'll see it every day. Such as an office or living area. Look at it any chance you get. You'll find over time all these things will come true for you.

Affirmations

Affirmations are uplifting phrases about yourself that will be repeated out loud until you change your mindset.

Your mind will believe things that you tell it.

We want to fill our minds with things that we want to bring into our lives.

Make a list of things that may not be true, but you want

to come true. For example, some of mines are:

- I am beautiful

- I am confident

- I am in a top earner in my company

- I am intelligent

- I am a great wife, sister, and daughter

- I am successful

- I am financially free

- I sponsor people effortlessly

- I vacation once a month

- I have free time to do whatever

- I am a multimillionaire

- I change people's lives for the better

- I am an action taker

- I own my own dream house and car

- I am a speaker and author

So what do you want to be? Write down your list or put it in your phone, somewhere where you'll have access to it.

Read your affirmations in the mirror every single day when you wake up and before you go to bed.

Look yourself in the eyes, this is you changing.

Chapter 6: Take Action Now

So enough talking, let's get to work. You learned how to set goals and stay motivated.

No longer allow your mindset to get in your way. Get uncomfortable-- this means you're growing.

Listen to plenty of audio that will feed your brain with the right stuff. Sometimes motivational music will even do the trick.

Do whatever it takes. Be committed and ever give up!

Always be reading the latest books on network marketing and take all the training you can to learn the industry.

Remember that in to attract people, you must share what you know and what you have learned.

Apply what you learned immediately. Keep investing in yourself and your dreams.

Constantly watch YouTube videos that are motivational and uplifting.

Keep learning and never stop growing.

Refer to your goals daily. Work toward your goals daily by doing you daily routine.

Constantly refer to your affirmations every morning and every night.

You have what it takes to be successful and it's always been in you. Once you realize you're good enough you will prosper.

Learning is great. Many of your competitors are still in the learning stage. Only a small percentage take action.

Be the one that takes action. Be the doer! Be an inspiration to yourself, your team, and your family.

When people think of you, they should think of success, hard work, and commitment.

Today is better than any to get started. For as long as you live, it's ever too late to change.

Conclusion

Thank you again for reading *Network Marketing Mindset*!

I hope this book was able to help you to gain confidence and grow your business.

The next step is to get started mapping out your goals for the month and find an accountability partner.

Finally, if you enjoyed this book, then I'd like to ask you for a favor, would you be kind enough to leave a review for this book on Amazon? It'd be greatly appreciated!

By leaving a review, you'll help others to find the book. It will also give me feedback on what I can improve, and what I've done well.

Thank you and good luck!